D1169611

THE TEN COMMANDMENTS

*12 studies
for individuals or groups*

Rob Suggs

With Notes for Leaders

InterVarsity Press
Downers Grove, Illinois

InterVarsity Press
P.O. Box 1400, Downers Grove, IL 60515-1426
World Wide Web: www.ivpress.com
E-mail: mail@ivpress.com

©*1997, 2002 by Rob Suggs*

InterVarsity Press® *is the book-publishing division of InterVarsity Christian Fellowship/USA*®*, a student movement active on campus at hundreds of universities, colleges and schools of nursing in the United States of America, and a member movement of the International Fellowship of Evangelical Students. For information about local and regional activities, write Public Relations Dept., InterVarsity Christian Fellowship/USA, 6400 Schroeder Rd., P.O. Box 7895, Madison, WI 53707-7895, or visit the IVCF website at <www.ivcf.org>.*

LifeGuide® *is a registered trademark of InterVarsity Christian Fellowship.*

All Scripture quotations, unless otherwise indicated, are taken from the Holy Bible, New International Version®*.* NIV®*. Copyright* ©*1973, 1978, 1984 by International Bible Society. Used by permission of Zondervan Publishing House. All rights reserved.*

Cover photograph: Dennis Flaherty

ISBN 0-8308-3084-7

Printed in the United States of America ∞

P	18	17	16	15	14	13	12	11	10	9	8	7	6	5	4
Y	17	16	15	14	13	12	11	10	09	08	07	06	05		

Contents

Getting the Most Out of
The Ten Commandments

In Bill Watterson's comic strip, Calvin and Hobbes, Calvin challenges Hobbes the tiger to an outdoor game. He hits a grounder, only to find Hobbes has beaten him to first base. Undaunted, the boy turns and sprints for third, or he quickly creates a new base. Maybe he punts. All's fair in "Calvinball," a chaotic competition in which rules are spontaneous and unbinding.

Watterson has retired his comic strip. But here in the real world, many of us are playing out our own versions of "Calvinball." Rules are recognized and affirmed—until they become inconvenient. What absolute principles govern business endeavors? Is marriage really "'til death do us part"? After a few rounds of the game, we begin to wonder if rules are such a bad thing after all. We begin to yearn for simple, value-enriched guidelines for living. The problem: Who writes the rules and marks the boundaries?

Thousands of years ago, the people of God found themselves at a similar crossroad in the wilderness. Behind them lay slavery and degradation, ahead gleamed the promise of freedom and prosperity. All things seemed possible—including loss of direction, starvation and exposure. Some of them began to have second thoughts about this freedom idea. After all, slavery had its points: security, for one. Freedom, once acquired, can be terrifying.

At this defining moment, Moses climbed a mountain to seek the answers from the God who had provided the freedom. When he descended, he carried in his hands and heart a concise declaration of wisdom for the ages. We know it as the Ten Commandments, though the Old Testament speaks of the "Ten Words."

Are these the boundaries we crave? Yes, but they are much more than that. These are rules that restrict, yet give freedom. They are words of prevention, but also protection. They are both fundamental and profound, inner-directed and outward-reaching. God gave us ten words that establish identity: ours and his. The Ten Commandments constitute a "Declaration of Dependence." They affirm our dependence on God and each other.

Some years ago, a well-known media magnate issued his own update of the commandments. The old, "negative" ones, he declared had become so much religious baggage. He offered the world an alternative list of ten politically correct "affirmations" to replace the dreary old commandments. Cullen Murphy, writing in *The Atlantic Monthly,* observed that "suggestions for replacing the Ten Commandments altogether are, in fact, becoming common" ("Broken Covenant?" November 1996, pp. 22-24). Not too surprisingly, these updates fail to catch on. It turns out that people are drawn to those dusty words engraved on the courthouse door. They are willing to affirm that such acts as killing and stealing are, yes, "negative."

The commandments retain their power. As a matter of fact, you might be surprised by their everyday relevance. The stones on which God's finger etched the commandments are lost, but the words live on, for our own hearts bear his fingerprints. Ten words mark the starting point to knowing God and living in society, but they lead us to yet another crossroad, where law ends and grace begins.

On the way, however, there is a mountain to climb. Alongside Moses, we seek God's face, and our prayer is to receive the Word of Life clearly and eagerly. Like Moses, we will come away from the encounter with glowing faces, and people will know at a glance that we have encountered not just God's laws but God himself.

Suggestions for Individual Study

1. As you begin each study, pray that God will speak to you through his Word.

2. Read the introduction to the study and respond to the personal reflection question or exercise. This is designed to help you focus on God and on the theme of the study.

3. Each study deals with a particular passage—so that you can delve into the author's meaning in that context. Read and reread the passage to be studied. The questions are written using the language of the New International Version, so you may wish to use that version of the Bible. The New Revised Standard Version is also recommended.

4. This is an inductive Bible study, designed to help you discover for yourself what Scripture is saying. The study includes three types of questions. *Observation* questions ask about the basic facts: who, what, when, where and how. *Interpretation* questions delve into the meaning of the passage. *Application* questions help you discover the implications of the text for growing in Christ. These three keys unlock the treasures of Scripture.

Write your answers to the questions in the spaces provided or in a personal journal. Writing can bring clarity and deeper understanding of yourself and of God's Word.

5. It might be good to have a Bible dictionary handy. Use it to look up any unfamiliar words, names or places.

6. Use the prayer suggestion to guide you in thanking God for what you have learned and to pray about the applications that have come to mind.

7. You may want to go on to the suggestion under "Now or Later," or you may want to use that idea for your next study.

Suggestions for Members of a Group Study

1. Come to the study prepared. Follow the suggestions for individual study mentioned above. You will find that careful preparation will greatly enrich your time spent in group discussion.

2. Be willing to participate in the discussion. The leader of your group will not be lecturing. Instead, he or she will be encouraging the members of the group to discuss what they have learned. The leader will be asking the questions that are found in this guide.

3. Stick to the topic being discussed. Your answers should be based on the verses which are the focus of the discussion and not on outside authorities such as commentaries or speakers. These studies focus on a particular passage of Scripture. Only rarely should you refer to other portions of the Bible. This allows for everyone to participate in in-depth study on equal ground.

4. Be sensitive to the other members of the group. Listen attentively when they describe what they have learned. You may be surprised by their insights! Each question assumes a variety of answers. Many questions do not have "right" answers, particularly questions that aim at meaning or application. Instead the questions push us to explore the passage more thoroughly.

When possible, link what you say to the comments of others. Also, be affirming whenever you can. This will encourage some of the more hesitant members of the group to participate.

5. Be careful not to dominate the discussion. We are sometimes so eager to express our thoughts that we leave too little opportunity for others to respond. By all means participate! But allow others to also.

6. Expect God to teach you through the passage being discussed and through the other members of the group. Pray that you will have an enjoyable and profitable time together, but also that as a result of the study you will find ways that you can take action individually and/or as a group.

7. Remember that anything said in the group is considered confidential and should not be discussed outside the group unless specific permission is given to do so.

8. If you are the group leader, you will find additional suggestions at the back of the guide.

1

Laying Down
the Law

Exodus 20

It's tough being a child. At every turn there are new laws: the "law of crossing the street," the "law of speaking and interrupting." Then there is the complex maze of the "dinner table law." Childhood is marked by hearing and understanding instruction. If we accept and follow these customs, we become capable, functioning adults.

GROUP DISCUSSION. Think back to when you were a child or a teen. Give an example of a time you obeyed your parents' rules, even though your parents weren't around.

PERSONAL REFLECTION. Why does keeping the commandments of God require faith?

The book of Exodus describes the childhood of Israel. The descendants of Abraham, Isaac and Jacob, who settled in Egypt, had become slaves. Under the leadership of Moses and his brother Aaron, and through God's miracles, they managed an escape. The book of Exodus (which means "departure" or "exit") lays the foundation of God's Old

Testament revelation about himself: his name, his requirements and how he is to be worshiped. The focal point of this revelation is the giving of the law to Moses at Mount Sinai.

We are accustomed to hearing the Ten Commandments in church and seeing them on stone monuments. Perhaps you had to recite them when you were confirmed or joined the church. *Read Exodus 19:16-19* to bring the original setting to life.

1. What would you have seen and heard if you had been there?

2. *Read Exodus 20.* As you hear the law delivered, what stands out to you?

3. How does God establish his right to issue these commands to the Israelites (v. 2)?

4. What is the unifying theme of the first four commands (vv. 3-11)?

5. Why is it appropriate that these four commands should come first?

6. Focus on the picture of God in the first four commandments. How might you need to adjust your image of God to fit with what these commands tell us about who God is?

---

7. How does the commandment to honor parents (v. 12) serve as a "hinge" between the first four and the final five commandments?

---

8. What logic do you find in the order of the final five commandments in verses 13-17?

---

9. The Israelites fall back in fear from the manifestations of God's presence (vv. 18-19). Moses tells them "Do not be afraid," then goes on to express the hope that the "fear of God" will stay with them (v. 20). How do you resolve the apparent contradiction in Moses' words?

---

10. How exactly is God testing the Israelites (v. 20)?

---

11. Given what the people have experienced, why is a sacrifice appropriate (v. 24)?

12. Which of the Ten Commandments presents the greatest challenge to you right now?

---

13. Based on these commandments, what is one way in which you sense God calling you to be more obedient in the coming week, and how will you obey?

"If we claim to be without sin, we deceive ourselves and the truth is not in us. If we confess our sins, he is faithful and just and will forgive us our sins and purify us from all unrighteousness" (1 John 1:8-9). In a time of quietness, pray for God's forgiveness in Christ. Ask for grace to keep these laws in your heart as well as externally. Thank God for his mercy.

Now or Later

Consider how the Ten Commandments reveal the character of God. Write a psalm of praise for who God is, as these commandments reveal him.

What changes would you like to see in your life as this study of the commandments unfolds? Make this a matter of reflection and prayer.

2

The One & Only

1 Kings 18:16-39

Which investment strategy is right for me? How can I stay healthy and live a long life? Who has the solution to my emotional problems? Where can I find peace and success? There is no shortage of gurus to advise us in every area of life. We can choose among a vast assortment of health gurus, fitness gurus, investment gurus, technology gurus, self-help gurus and, presumably, gurus of guruism. But sometimes gurus collide: which has the best diet plan or career-path strategy? It's your call.

The first commandment simplifies things. Its message is this: Follow the Leader—the only Leader.

GROUP DISCUSSION. In Exodus 20:3 God says, "You shall have no other gods before me." The first commandment could not be simpler, and humanity has found a million ways to break it. Almost anything can be a god. From your observation, what gods are the most popular today?

PERSONAL REFLECTION. What false gods compete most for your loyalty to the one true God (Exodus 20:3)?

After King Solomon died, his kingdom split into the two kingdoms of Israel and Judah. Each had a succession of kings, many of whom rebelled against God and led the people into idolatry. One of the worst was Ahab, king of Israel. The prophet Elijah boldly stood up to Ahab. During a severe drought, Elijah confronted the prophets of the fertility god Baal, who were supported by Ahab's wife Jezebel. *Read 1 Kings 18:16-39.*

1. Contrast the general mood and attitude of Elijah with the mood and attitude of the followers of Baal throughout this passage.

2. Ahab calls Elijah "you troubler of Israel" (v. 17). What does that reveal about his frame of mind?

3. For his confrontation, Elijah deliberately chooses Mount Carmel, a location commonly used for the worship of Baal—in other words, Baal's own "turf" (v. 19). Why is this a strategic choice?

4. What are some possible contexts ("turfs") in which the gods of this world can be confronted and challenged today?

5. What risks does Elijah take by calling for a public confrontation (vv. 19-20)?

6. The Hebrew term translated "waver" can also mean "to limp" (v. 21). What does Elijah mean by his accusation of wavering?

7. Elijah employs historic symbolism in building an altar (vv. 31-32). Why is this important?

8. How has your own spiritual history given you courage in times of testing?

9. Water would be a precious commodity during a drought. Why would Elijah make a show of pouring it repeatedly over an altar built for fire (vv. 33-34)?

10. How do verses 36 and 37 reveal that this confrontation will not be just a show of power?

11. How does God answer Elijah, and with what results (vv. 38-39)?

12. Humanly speaking, the odds were definitely against Elijah. It was 450 to 1, not to mention 400 others in verse 19, plus Ahab and

Jezebel! Identify some of the many "prophets of Baal" who surround you as you try to serve God.

---

13. Dramatic showdowns such as in this Scripture passage are (thankfully) rare. However, we all have frequent, even daily, showdowns where we are called to challenge idolatry. How have you seen God show his power in those situations?

Pray that you will be single-minded and will serve God with your whole heart. Pray for those who are bound in the futility of idols and for those who need to make up their minds who they will serve.

Now or Later
Who do you know who is "limping" or "wavering" between the true God and idolatry?

How can you encourage that person to choose the right way?

Write an imaginary confrontation that could take place if Elijah lived in your culture today. What would be the present-day Mount Carmel? Who is Baal and who are his prophets? Who are Ahab and Jezebel? How would the confrontation take place? What would you title it?

3

Idol Minds

Vince finally owns it: the ultimate automobile. Ever since he spotted that certain make and model three years ago, he has been obsessed with making one his own—despite a modest income. After long, tiring months and a second job, the down payment became a reality. Vince is so proud and protective he is almost afraid to take the car out in traffic. He loves to wash it, wax it and sit behind the wheel just to hear the wonderful sound of the car idling—or is that idoling?

GROUP DISCUSSION. Describe an acquisition you once desired more than anything in the world and what happened when you got it.

PERSONAL REFLECTION. What is a possession you wish you had, and why? What is a possession you have and wish you didn't, and why?

In Exodus 20:4-6, God speaks the second commandment:

> You shall not make for yourself an idol in the form of anything in heaven above or on the earth beneath or in the waters below. You shall not bow down to them or worship them; for I, the Lord your God, am

a jealous God, punishing the children for the sin of the fathers to the third and fourth generation of those who hate me, but showing love to a thousand generations of those who love me and keep my commandments.

1. What is the difference between the first commandment ("no other gods before me") and the second?

2. Why might this sin (as well as its avoidance) affect future generations (vv. 5-6)?

3. While Moses was on Mount Sinai receiving the law of God, events at the foot of the mountain took a shocking turn. *Read Exodus 32.* This series of events appears to take place over two days and nights. What are the key points of decision by Aaron and the people during this time?

4. What apparently causes the Israelites to yearn for new gods (32:1)?

5. When have you experienced yearnings similar to those of the Israelites?

6. How did Aaron attempt to mix idolatry and the worship of God (32:5-6)?

7. God had every right to wipe out the idolatrous people (32:7-10). Why did Moses intervene with God on behalf of the Israelites (32:11-14)?

8. When Moses sees the people's idolatry, he reacts in anger (32:19-20). Why does idolatry anger God's faithful people?

9. Moses is concerned that the people have become "a laughingstock to their enemies" (32:25). What messages do believers send through idol worship and its consequences?

---

10. The consequences of Israelite unfaithfulness are severe (32:27-29), in keeping with the detailed warning of the commandment (20:4-6). Why do you think this particular violation so offends God?

---

11. What potential "golden calves" threaten to steal our allegiance today?

---

12. Moses immediately destroyed the golden calf (32:20). What idols need to be confronted in your own life?

Pray for wisdom and courage to emulate Moses in your relationship with God and in your care for sinning people.

Now or Later

The Israelites had to face the truth and swallow the remains of their own false god (32:20). No doubt the taste was bitter, but it brought them back to reality. In a private journal entry, confess areas of your life where you might serve a false god even while appearing to serve Christ. Commit yourself to the Lord in a fresh way, and thank him for his mercy.

4

Respect for the Name

Once there was a young, shy boy from Chicago who wanted to be a cartoonist. He managed to create the first "talking" cartoon short, "Steamboat Willie," from which a star emerged: Mickey Mouse. But when you hear the name Walt Disney today, you probably don't think of the man who died in 1966. You think of classic cartoons. You think of an entertainment empire. The name has outlived its owner and taken on a life of its own. The third commandment is based on the power of a name.

GROUP DISCUSSION. What do you know about the history and meaning of your name?

PERSONAL REFLECTION. If you could change your first name, what would you change it to, and why?

Exodus 20:7 gives the third commandment: "You shall not misuse the name of the Lord your God, for the Lord will not hold anyone guiltless who misuses his name."

1. What are some common misuses of the Lord's name?

2. How would you explain the difference, if any, between this commandment and profanity?

3. How does the third commandment build on the first two?

4. In the psalms, the Lord's name appears over and over and is always honored. *Read Psalm 96.* In a word or a phrase, what is the theme of this psalm?

5. What response does this psalm raise in you, particularly as you read it aloud?

6. How do we know that the writer of Psalm 96 did not take the Lord's name lightly?

7. Why would we praise God's name, as opposed to simply praising God (v. 2)?

8. Verses 3-5 speak of declaring God's glory to the nations, particularly to those who worship idols. How should evangelism and missions influence us in the proper use of God's name?

9. How can we ascribe to God (and thus to his name) glory and strength (v. 7)?

10. How does making an offering give glory to God's name (v. 8)?

11. Verses 10-13 deal with the natural world. When has nature contributed to your praise of God's name?

12. When you hear God's name misused, how do you react?

13. How can you respond to the misuse of God's name in a way that honors God and does not simply condemn others?

Spend a period of time reflecting on the glory of God's name. Make a commitment to declare his glory in the coming week. Pray for forgiveness for any wrong use of his name.

Now or Later

You have reflected on the words *God* and *Lord*. By what other names do you know God in all three of his Persons? Write as many names as you can recall. Search through the Scriptures for others. Choose one or two favorite names, and explain why they have particular meaning for you.

5

Respect for Sabbath Rest

Psalm 16

The Scottish runner Eric Liddell had waited his whole life to run one race. But as the world watched in shock, he withdrew his name. Olympic organizers had scheduled the qualifying heat on a Sunday. As a Christian, Liddell felt he would dishonor God by participating on that day. However, God honored Eric Liddell's faithfulness, and he was able to win a gold medal in another event.

Would you have done the same? Few of us hold the sabbath in such regard today.

GROUP DISCUSSION. Describe a typical Sunday in the home in which you grew up. What (if anything) set that day apart from the other days of the week?

PERSONAL REFLECTION. Write out your typical Sunday routine. Other than going to church, how is your Sunday different from other days of the week, and why?

Read the fourth commandment in Exodus 20:8-11:

> Remember the Sabbath day by keeping it holy. Six days you shall labor and do all your work, but the seventh day is a Sabbath to the Lord your God. On it you shall not do any work, neither you, nor your son or daughter, nor your manservant or maidservant, nor your animals, nor the alien within your gates. For in six days the Lord made the heavens and the earth, the sea, and all that is in them, but he rested on the seventh day. Therefore the Lord blessed the Sabbath day and made it holy.

1. What does the explanation for this commandment imply about the relationship between God and humanity?

2. What do you think it means to keep the sabbath holy?

3. *Read Psalm 16,* a psalm of David. What moods does David express throughout this psalm?

4. What are some of the psalmist's sources of delight (vv. 2-7)?

5. As David considers his life, which observations help him find peace with his "lot in life" (vv. 5-6)?

6. How do God's presence and teaching affect the psalmist (vv. 7-8)?

7. What are examples of ways you have found rest by "practicing the presence of God"?

8. How does David face the uncertainty of the future (vv. 9-10)?

9. How does observance of the sabbath help you find rest in the Lord?

10. What do Christians lose by treating Sunday as just another day of the week?

11. In Psalm 16, David does not specifically refer to the sabbath; yet the entire psalm radiates an attitude of rest in the Lord. How would you summarize the way David reached this point of rest?

12. Looking back over Psalm 16 as a whole, what is most important to people who follow God?

How do those values contrast with worldly values?

13. What arrangements (or rearrangements) will you make to better keep the sabbath holy and give yourself opportunity for needed rest?

Bring to mind the issues in your life that keep you from rest. Pray that you would "set the Lord always before [you]" this week, that your "body also will rest secure" (Psalm 16:8-9).

Now or Later

Agree with friends or other members of your group to take steps to keep Sunday as a true day of rest. The point is not to lay down laws for each other but to encourage each other to think more carefully about the use of Sundays and to change harmful patterns into healthy ones.

6

Respect for Parents

Ruth 1:1-18

When we speak of the Sandwich Generation, we are talking not about diets but about demographics. These days young adults tend to start their own families later in life, while their own parents are living longer. The result? The middle group finds itself "sandwiched" between caring for the two adjacent generations—their aging parents and their own children.

Being the center of a sandwich does not seem an enviable position. Yet the Bible consistently teaches veneration of the elderly. In particular, God says we are blessed when we honor our parents, no matter what their age. Even if they are not living, we can honor their memory.

GROUP DISCUSSION. Consider this question: "Other than life, what was the best gift your parents ever gave you?" How might you have answered that question at age ten or fifteen, and how has your answer changed (if it has)?

PERSONAL REFLECTION. How has your attitude toward your parents changed and matured over the years?

Exodus 20:12 reads, "Honor your father and your mother, so that you may live long in the land the Lord your God is giving you."

1. The final six commandments govern human relationships. Why do you think this particular one would be found at the top of them?

2. Most of us have some mixed feelings about this commandment. How do you respond to it?

3. Notice the words "that you may live long." Do you believe this commandment in fact promises longevity for those who respect their parents? Explain your response.

4. *Read Ruth 1:1-18.* While Naomi and Ruth are not related by birth, what factors would contribute to their acting as parent and child?

5. For what reasons would Naomi dismiss her daughters-in-law and choose to travel alone (vv. 8-9)?

6. Describe Naomi's spiritual outlook at this time in her life (v. 13).

———————————————————————————

7. Imagine yourself as Orpah at the point of verse 14. How do you differ from Ruth in your view of Naomi and your outlook on the future?

———————————————————————————

8. What sacrifices does Ruth make in her commitment to stay with Naomi (vv. 16-17)?

———————————————————————————

9. What fears or anxieties have you faced concerning sacrifices you may need to make for your parents?

———————————————————————————

10. Ruth made a firm commitment to Naomi (vv. 16-17). How is it beneficial to verbalize our loyalty to our parents?

———————————————————————————

11. As the story plays out, Ruth marries (and finds a place in the ancestry of Jesus); Naomi becomes a "grandmother" (see 4:13-17). What are some rewards of being faithful to our parents?

12. What are some (perhaps conflicting) ways our culture views elderly people?

13. If your parents are living, what are three ways you can express your love and commitment to them? (If your parents aren't living, then think of some other elderly relative or friend.)

Pray for older people in your church and community. Ask for peace, physical strength and safety, provision of physical needs and companionship.

Now or Later

Plan a way your group can minister to an older person or older people in a practical way: help with a project around the house, a nursing home visit, offering rides, even committing yourselves to phoning regularly to check on someone. Keep in mind that it is better to make a small commitment and keep it than to overcommit and then fade away.

Ask family members if there are particular areas where your group could help. Don't be afraid to ask whether your help would be welcome; some older people may see it as an infringement on their independence, while others will appreciate your concern.

7

Respect for Life

1 Samuel 24

Shootings in our public schools have raised questions about the effects on our children of violence in our entertainment. Is it healthy to let children roam virtual corridors armed with virtual assault weapons, blowing away hordes of enemies until killing becomes a casual matter? Time will tell how deeply our attitudes toward violence have changed. The sixth commandment is plain and simple: "You shall not murder." The Scriptures teach us to choose life.

GROUP DISCUSSION. Why do you think people find the subject of murder (in novels, movies and news items, for instance) so intriguing?

PERSONAL REFLECTION. Of all the crimes human beings can commit, why is murder considered the worst?

The sixth commandment says, "You shall not murder" (Exodus 20:13).

---

1. The Hebrew version of verses 13-15 contains only two words per commandment: the equivalent of "No murder. No adultery. No stealing." How would you describe the general effect of such terse language?

2. *Read 1 Samuel 24*. What is the progression of events in this vivid narrative?

3. How do David's "friends" encourage him to take advantage of the situation in the cave (v. 4)?

4. If you had been one of David's companions, what would you have thought of him for sparing his enemy Saul?

5. How might David have rationalized the killing of Saul?

6. Why is David's conscience stricken after he cuts off Saul's robe (vv. 5-7)?

7. Besides his refusal to kill Saul, how does David show respect for Saul's life (vv. 8-13)?

8. What peacemaking strategies does David use in verses 8-13?

9. In verses 14-15 David belittles himself as a target of Saul's wrath. What is the relationship between humility and respect for life?

10. What effect does David's mercy have on Saul (vv. 16-22)?

11. What new insight does Saul verbalize regarding the cyclical nature of killing and vengeance (vv. 16-21)?

12. How have David and Saul affected their future prospects by their exchange at the cave?

13. While few of us find ourselves in situations quite like David's at the cave, we have people who are "out to get us." Sometimes we see opportunities to harm and even destroy those people. What does this Scripture have to say to us when those openings arise?

Pray that you will take a stand for the biblical value of life no matter where or how you see it threatened.

Now or Later

This study provides an open door for peacemaking. Recall how David's respect for Saul's life went far beyond refraining from murder. Consider ways to build better relationships, as far as you are able, with any people you feel are "out to get you." Here Paul's words in Romans 12:18 offer encouragement: "If it is possible, as far as it depends on you, live at peace with everyone."

Make a separate study of Matthew 5:21-22, in which Jesus interprets the command "You shall not murder" to include attacks on a person's character. Consider ways in which you are tempted to make verbal attacks on others (including the indirect attacks of gossip).

8

Respect for Marriage

The book *Sex in America* reports that 20 percent of all women and as many as 35 percent of all men have been unfaithful in marriage. *Christianity Today* surveyed its readers and discovered that 23 percent of their subscribers admitted to having had affairs. *Leadership Journal* found that 10 percent of the pastors and church leaders they surveyed had committed adultery. Can something so common be so wrong? The seventh commandment says yes, it can.

GROUP DISCUSSION. What factors do you think contribute to widespread adultery in our times?

PERSONAL REFLECTION. When has adultery (actual or imagined) presented a temptation for you? How did your faith in God affect your response to temptation?

Exodus 20:14 gives the seventh commandment: "You shall not commit adultery."

1. What does adultery have in common with previous commandments?

2. *Read 2 Samuel 11.* In contrast to David's situation in the preceding study, he is now secure in his reign and lives in a luxurious palace in Jerusalem. What are the escalation points in this tragic drama, at which David makes each new decision?

3. What do we learn about David's character from the unfolding strategy of his adultery, attempted cover-up and murder?

4. Why do adultery and deceit naturally accompany each other?

5. In what kinds of circumstances are you likely to fail to be honest with yourself and God?

6. Contrast Uriah's character and behavior with that of David (vv. 9-13).

7. How does David's sin "ripple" outward to corrupt others?

8. What do David's actions in verses 22-27 reveal about how he felt about the situation?

9. We know that David was generally righteous and even "a man after God's own heart" (1 Samuel 13:14). How do you account for his behavior?

10. Which of the Ten Commandments has David violated in the course of this chapter?

11. What is our responsibility in the avoidance of adultery?

---

12. What steps will you take to avoid compromising your own purity?

Pray for protection and wisdom in the area of sexual temptation. Pray for those caught or in danger of being caught (without naming names if you are in a group) in the destructive spiral of sexual sin.

Now or Later

Make a separate study of Matthew 5:27-30. In this part of the Sermon on the Mount, Jesus expands the command "You shall not commit adultery" to include the covetous look and thought. In what ways might this be an issue in your life?

9

Respect for Property

Jan is happily pecking away at the keyboard. Armed with brand new financial software, she finds great satisfaction in computing her income, paying her bills and anticipating her expenses. The software itself was not an expense; a friend let Jan copy it from his disk. So this program was free, and Jan calls that good money management!

The software manufacturer would call it something else. Jan knows that. Surely they expect a certain amount of "bootlegging," right? Don't they figure all that into their budgets?

GROUP DISCUSSION. Describe an incident when you were the victim of theft. How did you feel, and what did you do as a result?

PERSONAL REFLECTION. When have you been tempted to steal something? What was the outcome?

Exodus 20:15, the eighth commandment, says, "You shall not steal."

1. How many varieties of stealing can you name?

2. *Read Acts 4:32—5:11.* What was the importance and place of possessions in this early Christian community?

3. What is the relationship between sharing possessions and sharing the gospel (4:33)?

4. Describe the impact the believers had on their local economy (4:34-35).

How could the church today follow such a model?

5. What actions of Ananias and Sapphira brought about Peter's (and God's) wrath (5:1-2)?

6. Do you believe this passage negates the concept of personal ownership for Christians? Explain your response.

7. How would you describe your attitude toward your own possessions? (And how satisfied are you with your attitude?)

8. How does Peter show Ananias his sin in a different perspective (5:3-4)?

9. Ananias and Sapphira actually die as judgment for their sin (5:5-11). Why might the punishment be so severe?

10. What are some ways Christians might steal from the church today?

11. What possession(s) do you guard most carefully, and why?

12. How can your most cherished possessions be used to further God's glory?

Pray for the right attitude toward possessions. Thank God for what you have. Ask him for a spirit of generosity to share with others in need.

Now or Later
Write a story or drama to answer this question: If a fellow Christian said he or she needed something of yours, how would you respond?

10

Respect for the Truth

"What's so funny?" Dad asks his giggling children.

"We're trying to find out which of us has told the biggest whopper."

"When I was a kid, I never even thought about telling a lie," Dad replies.

The children whisper, then one speaks up. "I guess that's it. Dad's the winner!"

In our world, honesty is more remarkable than lies. We're accustomed to "whoppers" in advertising, politics and polite society. We make jokes about the lies of lawyers and car dealers. We expect dishonesty from nearly everyone. The ninth commandment speaks to the issue of truth-telling.

GROUP DISCUSSION. Describe an occasion (perhaps as a child or teenager) when you were caught in a lie.

PERSONAL REFLECTION. Who is the most truthful person you know? What do you like about him or her?

Exodus 20:16 gives the ninth commandment: "You shall not give false testimony against your neighbor."

1. Compare lying, in its nature and consequences, to some of the other commandments.

2. Proverbs 12 repeatedly deals with the subject of honesty. *Read Proverbs 12:5-7.* What is the main theme of these three sayings?

3. How can honest words rescue someone (v. 6)?

4. *Read Proverbs 12:13-14.* What kinds of traps can sinful talk set for us?

5. How can mere words fill us with good things (v. 14)?

What does "the work of [our] hands" have to do with this principle?

6. *Read Proverbs 12:17-23.* The writer intermingles sayings about lying and reckless speech. What do they have in common?

7. Is it possible for someone to be reckless by being honest? Explain.

8. What kinds of reckless speech are tempting to you?

9. What point about honesty and lying is made in verse 19?

10. Of all sins, lying is the one most identified with the devil ("father

of lies," John 8:44). Why do you think this is so?

---

11. Verse 22 tells us God's response to lying and to truth. How can this affect our commitment to honesty?

---

12. How can you use words wisely to promote truth and peace this week?

We all like to think of ourselves as honest. Ask God to shine a searchlight into your heart and expose any areas of dishonesty, whether with yourself, with him or with others.

Now or Later

Make a commitment with someone else (or make it together as a group) to write down every lie you tell this week. Include "little white lies," deliberate whoppers and everything in between. You don't have to share them with each other; just write them down. At a later date, discuss what you learned about yourself through the experience.

11

The Value of Contentment

And so we come to the last word, the grand finale: You shall not covet.

That's it? Somehow this command seems out of place. Does coveting even belong on the same list with idolatry, murder, theft and adultery? After all, it is simply a "thought crime." It inflicts no damage on others. Or does it?

The tenth and final commandment, moving from action to thought, suggests new possibilities. It foreshadows a new law, one that will concern itself less with the hands than with the heart.

GROUP DISCUSSION. What is the difference between coveting and innocent desire?

PERSONAL REFLECTION. Do you think you are more fortunate or less fortunate than the people you know? Why do you feel this way?

Exodus 20:17, the tenth commandment, says this: "You shall not covet your neighbor's house. You shall not covet your neighbor's wife, or his manservant or maidservant, his ox or donkey, or anything that belongs to your neighbor."

1. Why do you think this commandment is placed last?

2. In your opinion, why does God include specific examples in this particular commandment?

3. *Read 1 Timothy 6:3-10.* Paul writes this letter to his young protégé Timothy, who had taken over leadership of the church at Ephesus (see 1:3). Paul wants to give Timothy practical advice about issues that are bound to arise in this church. What are some fundamental issues he addresses in this passage?

4. Given that the Proverbs teach that godly people often find material success, why is Paul so concerned about the teachings that threaten the Ephesian church (vv. 3-5)?

5. How would you define "godliness with contentment" (v. 6)?

6. Contentment implies a settled acceptance of what we already have. How can this be called *gain* (v. 6)?

7. Would you say that you have the contentment of verses 6-8? Why or why not?

8. Why does discontent breed covetousness?

9. How does our society actively promote discontent and covetousness?

10. To be content with food and clothing (v. 8) appears to rule out all other desires, such as for better physical comforts, health, personal advancement, education and other things people consider part of the good life. For a Christian, what is the place of these additional desires?

11. Paul warns of a trap that catches many (v. 9). How does this trap work?

12. Verse 10 is often misquoted as "Money is the root of all evil." How does the accurate reading help you understand God's view of money and ambition?

---

13. What are some "griefs" you have experienced or seen others experience from the love of money (v. 10)?

---

14. How can you more actively strive for "godliness with contentment" in your present situation?

Gratitude is an effective antidote (even a vaccine) against covetousness. Offer prayers of thanksgiving for the physical and spiritual gifts God has given you.

Now or Later
Draw your conception of the "trap" of verse 9. Then design an "escape hatch" for the trap (see v. 11 for ideas).

12

The Law of Grace

Romans 3:9-31

God's commandments are as applicable today as at any time in history. We affirm their truth and seek to walk in obedience, yet daily we stumble and fall.

Jesus said that he came not to abolish the law but to fulfill it (Matthew 5:17). His fulfillment of God's law carries us into a new relationship with the Lawgiver. This new relationship acknowledges the inevitability of our failure. It finds a new way to lift us up, dust us off and restore us once and for all. Through Christ, we discover the law of grace.

GROUP DISCUSSION. When have you felt that your best efforts weren't good enough?

PERSONAL REFLECTION. When have you been most grateful—and humbled—by another person's forgiveness?

The apostle Paul is writing to Gentile (non-Jewish) believers. Paul himself was trained as a Pharisee, a Jewish religious leader specially concerned about purity through the law. *Read Romans 3:9-31.*

1. What generalities does he draw about the righteousness of Jews and Gentiles?

---

2. In verses 10-18, Paul quotes from a variety of Old Testament passages. (Footnotes or cross-references in your Bible will help you look up the Old Testament sources.) Describe the picture of humanity that he constructs through these references.

---

3. Which of the Ten Commandments have been violated according to verses 10-18?

---

4. In what senses are the Jews both "under sin" (v. 9) and "under the law" (v. 19)?

---

5. How does the law make us conscious of sin (v. 20)?

6. When has Scripture brought home to you that a particular action or attitude was sin, though you previously excused it?

7. From verses 21-24, comment on the significance of each of these terms: *righteousness, justification, grace* and *redemption.*

8. For what purpose was Christ allowed to die (vv. 24-26)?

9. How are God's grace and justice related?

10. What is Paul saying about boasting (vv. 27-30)?

11. Why is the law not nullified by God's grace (v. 31)?

12. Given what we have learned about grace, how should we relate to the Ten Commandments?

13. What active response will you make to the loving grace of God?

Thank God for his law and for his forgiveness that covers your failures. Pray for those who are still trusting in their own righteousness, that they will see their need for Christ.

Now or Later

We all know people who do not profess to be Christians yet have high moral standards, perhaps even higher than some Christians! Often the most religious and respectable people have the most resistance to the gospel because they do not think they need it. Consider people you know who fit that description. How can you use their own high standards to introduce the idea that everyone needs a Savior?

Leader's Notes

Leading a Bible discussion can be an enjoyable and rewarding experience. But it can also be *scary*—especially if you've never done it before. If this is your feeling, you're in good company. When God asked Moses to lead the Israelites out of Egypt, he replied, "O Lord, please send someone else to do it"! (Ex 4:13). It was the same with Solomon, Jeremiah and Timothy, but God helped these people in spite of their weaknesses, and he will help you as well.

You don't need to be an expert on the Bible or a trained teacher to lead a Bible discussion. The idea behind these inductive studies is that the leader guides group members to discover for themselves what the Bible has to say. This method of learning will allow group members to remember much more of what is said than a lecture would.

These studies are designed to be led easily. As a matter of fact, the flow of questions through the passage from observation to interpretation to application is so natural that you may feel that the studies lead themselves. This study guide is also flexible. You can use it with a variety of groups—student, professional, neighborhood or church groups. Each study takes forty-five to sixty minutes in a group setting.

There are some important facts to know about group dynamics and encouraging discussion. The suggestions listed below should enable you to effectively and enjoyably fulfill your role as leader.

Preparing for the Study

1. Ask God to help you understand and apply the passage in your own life. Unless this happens, you will not be prepared to lead others. Pray too for the various members of the group. Ask God to open your hearts to the message of his Word and motivate you to action.

2. Read the introduction to the entire guide to get an overview of the

entire book and the issues which will be explored.

3. As you begin each study, read and reread the assigned Bible passage to familiarize yourself with it.

4. This study guide is based on the New International Version of the Bible. It will help you and the group if you use this translation as the basis for your study and discussion.

5. Carefully work through each question in the study. Spend time in meditation and reflection as you consider how to respond.

6. Write your thoughts and responses in the space provided in the study guide. This will help you to express your understanding of the passage clearly.

7. It might help to have a Bible dictionary handy. Use it to look up any unfamiliar words, names or places. (For additional help on how to study a passage, see chapter five of *How to Lead a LifeGuide Bible Study,* InterVarsity Press.)

8. Consider how you can apply the Scripture to your life. Remember that the group will follow your lead in responding to the studies. They will not go any deeper than you do.

9. Once you have finished your own study of the passage, familiarize yourself with the leader's notes for the study you are leading. These are designed to help you in several ways. First, they tell you the purpose the study guide author had in mind when writing the study. Take time to think through how the study questions work together to accomplish that purpose. Second, the notes provide you with additional background information or suggestions on group dynamics for various questions. This information can be useful when people have difficulty understanding or answering a question. Third, the leader's notes can alert you to potential problems you may encounter during the study.

10. If you wish to remind yourself of anything mentioned in the leader's notes, make a note to yourself below that question in the study.

Leading the Study

1. Begin the study on time. Open with prayer, asking God to help the group to understand and apply the passage.

2. Be sure that everyone in your group has a study guide. Encourage the group to prepare beforehand for each discussion by reading the introduction to the guide and by working through the questions in the study.

3. At the beginning of your first time together, explain that these studies are meant to be discussions, not lectures. Encourage the members of the group to participate. However, do not put pressure on those who may be hes-

itant to speak during the first few sessions. You may want to suggest the following guidelines to your group.

☐ Stick to the topic being discussed.

☐ Your responses should be based on the verses which are the focus of the discussion and not on outside authorities such as commentaries or speakers.

☐ These studies focus on a particular passage of Scripture. Only rarely should you refer to other portions of the Bible. This allows for everyone to participate in in-depth study on equal ground.

☐ Anything said in the group is considered confidential and will not be discussed outside the group unless specific permission is given to do so.

☐ We will listen attentively to each other and provide time for each person present to talk.

☐ We will pray for each other.

4. Have a group member read the introduction at the beginning of the discussion.

5. Every session begins with a group discussion question. The question or activity is meant to be used before the passage is read. The question introduces the theme of the study and encourages group members to begin to open up. Encourage as many members as possible to participate, and be ready to get the discussion going with your own response.

This section is designed to reveal where our thoughts or feelings need to be transformed by Scripture. That is why it is especially important not to read the passage before the discussion question is asked. The passage will tend to color the honest reactions people would otherwise give because they are, of course, supposed to think the way the Bible does.

You may want to supplement the group discussion question with an icebreaker to help people to get comfortable. See the community section of *Small Group Idea Book* for more ideas.

You also might want to use the personal reflection question with your group. Either allow a time of silence for people to respond individually or discuss it together.

6. Have a group member (or members if the passage is long) read aloud the passage to be studied. Then give people several minutes to read the passage again silently so that they can take it all in.

7. Question 1 will generally be an overview question designed to briefly survey the passage. Encourage the group to look at the whole passage, but try to avoid getting sidetracked by questions or issues that will be addressed later in the study.

8. As you ask the questions, keep in mind that they are designed to be used just as they are written. You may simply read them aloud. Or you may prefer to express them in your own words.

There may be times when it is appropriate to deviate from the study guide. For example, a question may have already been answered. If so, move on to the next question. Or someone may raise an important question not covered in the guide. Take time to discuss it, but try to keep the group from going off on tangents.

9. Avoid answering your own questions. If necessary, repeat or rephrase them until they are clearly understood. Or point out something you read in the leader's notes to clarify the context or meaning. An eager group quickly becomes passive and silent if they think the leader will do most of the talking.

10. Don't be afraid of silence. People may need time to think about the question before formulating their answers.

11. Don't be content with just one answer. Ask, "What do the rest of you think?" or "Anything else?" until several people have given answers to the question.

12. Acknowledge all contributions. Try to be affirming whenever possible. Never reject an answer. If it is clearly off-base, ask, "Which verse led you to that conclusion?" or again, "What do the rest of you think?"

13. Don't expect every answer to be addressed to you, even though this will probably happen at first. As group members become more at ease, they will begin to truly interact with each other. This is one sign of healthy discussion.

14. Don't be afraid of controversy. It can be very stimulating. If you don't resolve an issue completely, don't be frustrated. Move on and keep it in mind for later. A subsequent study may solve the problem.

15. Periodically summarize what the group has said about the passage. This helps to draw together the various ideas mentioned and gives continuity to the study. But don't preach.

16. At the end of the Bible discussion you may want to allow group members a time of quiet to work on an idea under "Now or Later." Then discuss what you experienced. Or you may want to encourage group members to work on these ideas between meetings. Give an opportunity during the session for people to talk about what they are learning.

17. Conclude your time together with conversational prayer, adapting the prayer suggestion at the end of the study to your group. Ask for God's help in following through on the commitments you've made.

18. End on time.

Many more suggestions and helps are found in *How to Lead a LifeGuide Bible Study*, which is part of the LifeGuide Bible Study series.

Components of Small Groups

A healthy small group should do more than study the Bible. There are four components to consider as you structure your time together.

Nurture. Small groups help us to grow in our knowledge and love of God. Bible study is the key to making this happen and is the foundation of your small group.

Community. Small groups are a great place to develop deep friendships with other Christians. Allow time for informal interaction before and after each study. Plan activities and games that will help you get to know each other. Spend time having fun together—going on a picnic or cooking dinner together.

Worship and prayer. Your study will be enhanced by spending time praising God together in prayer or song. Pray for each other's needs—and keep track of how God is answering prayer in your group. Ask God to help you to apply what you are learning in your study.

Outreach. Reaching out to others can be a practical way of applying what you are learning, and it will keep your group from becoming self-focused. Host a series of evangelistic discussions for your friends or neighbors. Clean up the yard of an elderly friend. Serve at a soup kitchen together, or spend a day working on a Habitat house.

Many more suggestions and helps in each of these areas are found in *Small Group Idea Book*. Information on building a small group can be found in *Small Group Leaders' Handbook* and *The Big Book on Small Groups* (both from Inter-Varsity Press). Reading through one of these books would be worth your time.

Study 1. Laying Down the Law. Exodus 20.

Purpose: To discover the setting in which God's law was given and take a preliminary glimpse at the Ten Commandments.

Background. The historical context in which the commandments were given is important. The journey of Exodus is more than physical; it is a spiritual journey as well. The two stone tablets, engraved by no less than God's finger, would later be carried through the desert by the Israelites in the ark of the covenant on their way to the land of promise. All Hebrew law ultimately derives from the commandments. Israel's sovereignty as a people is directly related to its dependence on God.

A brief commentary such as the *New Bible Commentary* or the notes in your study Bible will provide additional facts about Exodus and the commandments.

Question 2. This study gives an overview of the commandments. Avoid getting into a detailed discussion of each one. Remind group members that they will discuss each of the commandments in more detail as the study continues.

Question 3. God points out that he is the one to whom Israel owes its freedom. While the point may seem obvious, we often live in forgetfulness of the grace of God. "The saving action of Yahweh is the prior reality; grace is prior to law" (G. A. Buttrick, ed., *The Interpreter's Dictionary of the Bible* [Nashville: Abingdon, 1962], p. 569).

Questions 4-6. God's holiness is the subject of each of the first four commandments. He is the only God; he is beyond idols and images; his very name is holy; we are to keep one day holy in his honor. Group members might also recall Jesus' summary of these commandments: "Love the Lord your God with all your heart and with all your soul and with all your mind" (Mt 22:37). Either way, the emphasis is on God's uniqueness and absolute lordship.

Question 7. The fifth commandment, about honoring parents, is the transitional one. It is related to honoring God (the first four), as well as honoring our neighbor (the final five).

Question 8. The sixth commandment is the first purely social one, and we find it to be the most serious on a descending scale: murder, adultery, stealing, lying and coveting. All sin is serious, of course; the degree is established in the effect on others.

Respect for fellow humans is at the center of the final six commands. Each of these directives restrains us from abusing people and their possessions and setting ourselves up as gods. The social fabric is weakened and eventually torn when we do not show deference to one another.

Question 9. Moses did not want the people to be paralyzed with terror. He wanted them to be in such awe of God that they would take positive action to obey. A healthy fear is a positive reaction to the laws of God. This God who meets the Israelites at Mount Sinai is great enough to give and to enforce these laws. He is not a God to be taken lightly or approached casually. Fear in this situation means that the people are in awe of God and will obey him because of who he is.

Question 10. Testing is a frequent theme in Exodus. Children are often "tested" by their parents and by their teachers. The test shows whether a child is listening and learning. The Israelites, as God's children, are passing the test by showing an appropriate fear and awe for God's presence and power. Sometimes God must get our attention before we will hear him; at Mount Sinai the the thunder, smoke and lightning accomplish that purpose. **Question 11.** God has delivered to his people a code for living before him and in society. It is a grave moment in their history. It is natural and appropriate for the Israelites to show affection and dedication to their Lord through a sacrifice. The ritual also memorializes the moment in a concrete way. Note as well that burnt offerings and fellowship offerings are in keeping with the two kinds of commandments (God and society). Fellowship offerings are "better translated as 'communion meals'" (R. Alan Cole, *Exodus* [Downers Grove, Ill.: InterVarsity Press, 1973], p. 163). Finally, sacrifices were meant to atone for sin, which the commandments describe.

Question 12. This should remain a private question for each member to answer from his or her own conscience.

Study 2. The One & Only. 1 Kings 18:16-39.

Purpose: To better understand and exalt God as the one and only Lord and identify those concerns which compete for our commitment.

Question 2. The story of Elijah and Ahab, in which a true believer takes a tough stand for God in an age of spiritual drifting, carries relevance today. Ahab was a strong military leader but a weak moral guide, always in conflict with God's prophets. Like Ahab, the people nominally honored the Lord, but many were attracted to the pagan deity. Ahab's greeting to Elijah reflects the double-mindedness of Israel and perhaps an inner realization that the true God is displeased.

Question 3. "Baal was peculiarly the god of fertility. He controlled the seasons and was responsible for the storm and the rain. If a drought was upon the land, it was due to Baal's working. The devotee would appeal to him for relief of these conditions. With scorn, Elijah, on Mount Carmel, exposed the emptiness of this belief (1 Kings 18). If Baal failed, the God of Israel would not. At the word of Elijah, and in answer to his prayer, the rain came. There is another feature of this story. In the Hebrew text there are in fact two gods referred to in 1 Kings 18:19. These are Baal and Asherah (translated in the Authorized Version as 'the groves'). The documents excavated at Ugarit show us that Asherah was a female goddess, the consort of Baal, a sensuous, lustful creature" (J. A. Thompson, *The Bible and Archaeology*, 3rd ed. [Grand Rapids, Mich.: Eerdmans, 1982], p. 132). Asherah was represented by a sacred pole (see 1 Kings 15:11-13).

Since the land was under severe drought (see 17:1), Baal would seem the obvious deity to do something about it. Elijah chooses the one location where divine power would find, and impress, the most people. He is confident enough to take on Baal in Baal territory, even to drench an altar he intends to burn. Those who trust God's sovereignty display such confidence.

Question 4. False gods and their domains often provide the setting for God to reveal his power. Christians need to get out of the sanctuary and demonstrate the power of God in the marketplace, in schools and everywhere else false gods are revered.

Question 5. The prophets of Baal were in the pay of the king and queen. Baal himself was an empty idol, but Ahab and Jezebel had life-and-death power. Besides, Elijah was significantly outnumbered!

Question 6. People tend to be unfaithful to their gods, trying to have it both ways. Elijah challenges his people to have the courage of their convictions and determine once and for all who is really Lord.

The phrase meaning "to limp" is also used in verse 26 to describe the dance of the Baal prophets. Given Elijah's sarcastic bent, this is probably an intentional pun. Limping, of course, is trying to walk two different ways.

Question 7. Stone altars were often set up to commemorate an encounter with God (for example Gen 28:18 and 35:14). Elijah built an altar from twelve stones, one for each of the twelve tribes descended from the twelve sons of Jacob (Israel). These were the sons who went from Canaan to Egypt and whose descendants left Egypt in the exodus. In the Old Testament, God often calls himself "the God of Abraham, the God of Isaac and the God of Jacob" (for example, when he first appears to Moses, Ex 3:6). Our faith in God is partially built on God's past faithfulness. We receive inspiration and assurance from remembering what God has done for us and for others.

Question 9. Pouring out the water would have been a provocative act before onlookers. In one act Elijah illustrated his faith in God for both fire and rain.

Question 10. Elijah prays that God will show himself as God and that he, Elijah, will be vindicated; but he also expresses hope that the people's hearts will turn back to God.

Study 3. Idol Minds. Exodus 32.

Purpose: To define and combat idolatry in the lives of believers.

Question 1. The Puritan preacher Thomas Watson explained, "In the first commandment worshiping a false god is forbidden. In this, however, the second commandment, worshiping the true God in a false manner is forbidden" (As quoted in Stuart Briscoe, *The Ten Commandments* [Wheaton, Ill.: Shaw, 1993], p. 19). This command is also about trying to control God, whose transcendence cannot be captured in an image or icon.

In the second commandment, God calls himself "a jealous God." "'Zeal-ous' might be a better translation in modern English, since 'jealousy' has acquired an exclusively bad meaning. . . . 'Jealousy' does not refer to an emo-tion so much as to an activity, in this case an activity of violence and vehe-mence, that springs from the rupture of a personal bond as exclusive as that of the marriage bond. This is not therefore to be seen as intolerance but exclusiveness" (Cole, *Exodus*, p. 156). Thus, God is "jealous" as a spouse toward the marriage partner; no rivals will be tolerated. This truth takes in the first two commandments.

Question 2. The phrase "the third and fourth generations" is frequently used in the Old Testament. The Israelites recognized the domino effect of sin. In this case, false ideas of worship and the nature of God will particularly mis-lead and harm our children. Conversely, a home where God is loved will reward its descendants.

Question 3. The people get restless and approach Aaron to do something (v. 1). Aaron yields to their demands immediately (v. 2) and in an ongoing way (v. 4). The people give themselves over to pagan revelry in the name of wor-ship (v. 6). At any of these points the people or Aaron could have stopped themselves and recalled themselves and each other back to God. Their descent into idolatry is a series of choices.

Question 4. What the people wanted and expected from their God was not forthcoming. Their leader Moses had disappeared. They felt insecure and without direction. They wanted a tangible god who could provide them with what they thought they needed.

Question 6. Aaron appears to want to hedge his bets or have all the bases covered. He makes an idol, builds an altar and announces a festival to the Lord. The people proceed to offer sacrifices in front of the golden calf while apparently telling themselves that they are offering worship to God.

Question 7. Moses is concerned not only for the Israelites' reputation but for God's reputation among the nations. He appeals to God's promise to the Israel-ites' forefathers Abraham, Isaac and Jacob. See also his words in Exodus 33:16.

Question 9. From Abraham's covenant the Israelites were to represent and illuminate God in the world. In the same way, Christians must not sink to the world's standards. Mundane idolatry and "revelry" of any kind send a mes-sage about ourselves and the God we represent.

Question 10. Readers of the Old Testament naturally seek explanations of violent passages such as this one. God is concerned for keeping his people pure from the spread of outright disobedience and rebellion such as this. In general, idolatry is among the most destructive of sins. To spread a diminished, mundane idea of God is to poison the cultural air we breathe. To attempt to control God through idols is also a path to devastation. The Israelites, for example, finally found themselves sacrificing children to a god called Molech (see Lev 18:21; 20:3-5; Jer 32:35). As God is transcendent, it is imperative to keep our doctrine and worship of him pure. Also see Walter C. Kaiser, *Hard Sayings of the Old Testament* (Downers Grove, Ill.: InterVarsity Press, 1988), pp. 106-9.

Study 4. Respect for the Name. Psalm 96.
Purpose: To discover the holiness of God's name and be inspired to use it respectfully.
Question 1. Names are extremely important throughout Scripture. Abraham, Peter and Paul all bore changed names to reflect their changed identities. "In biblical times the name was considered an extension or expression of the person himself" (*The Revell Bible Dictionary,* ed. L. O. Richards [New York: Wynwood, 1990], p. 722). The Hebrew name of God (YHWH or Yahweh, "I Am Who I Am") was declared by God to Moses at the burning bush (Ex 3:14). This name was once considered far more sacred than it is today. Priests actually spoke it only once per year, on the Day of Atonement. Also, God's continuing presence and power were considered absolute, and to use his name casually was a blatant denial of that reality.

When the name LORD appears in your Bible in small capitals, it translates the Hebrew word Yahweh, "I Am." When the name appears as Lord, it translates the Hebrew word Adonai or "Lord."
Question 2. The first commandment deals with worshiping God only. "Whereas the second commandment prohibits visual representations of God, the third focuses on verbal representations" (*New Bible Commentary,* p. 107). Again, it implies an attempt to control God, this time by the use of his name.
Question 4. The *New Bible Commentary* entitles this psalm "The only God and his gospel." It calls on God's people to praise his name and to invite the nations to do so. Even the natural world is called on to issue praise to its Creator. The psalm ends in an evocation of God's future judgment in righteousness and truth.

Psalm 96 appears to be an excerpt from David's prayer of thanks when he brought the ark of God into the tent he had prepared for it in Jerusalem (1 Chron 16:23-33). The ark contained the Ten Commandments in stone, along with other items from the exodus (see Heb 9:4).
Question 5. It would be helpful to read the psalm aloud together as a group to get its full impact. Be sure everyone in the group has access to the same

translation before you read together.

Question 6. Psalm 96 is a psalm of large scope and worldwide themes. It sounds big, and we feel expansive as we read it. This is no trivial or casual praise for a good feeling.

Question 7. Of course we are actually praising God when we praise his name. To praise his name means to praise what we know of God. His name takes in his reputation and expression in the world, just as one's family name has a tradition attached to it.

Question 10. An offering is not limited to a church budget contribution. The possibilities for an offering are endless. The act of sacrifice heightens our awareness that God is more than worthy of our gift; it also reminds us of the ultimate sacrifice he made for us in Christ. Whenever we make any kind of offering, we should do so in his name, reflecting on it prayerfully.

Study 5. Respect for Sabbath Rest. Psalm 16.

Purpose: To consider God's institution of a cycle of work and rest, and the observance of the sabbath in God's honor.

Question 1. This commandment affirms that we are created in the image of God. He observed the seven-day work/rest cycle, and he ordains that we do so. Amidst the stern demands of the Ten Commandments, this directive provides a reminder that the commandments serve to protect us. As we ignore the command to rest, it can be no coincidence that our society experiences severe problems with stress and burnout.

Note that some Christians observe Saturday rather than Sunday as the sabbath. They believe Saturday observance to be more biblical, and indeed Saturday is the Jewish sabbath. Sunday began to take precedence as the Christian day of worship because Jesus rose from the dead early on Sunday morning.

Question 2. "The basic idea which the word *holy* expresses is that of separation, or separateness. When God is declared to be *holy,* the thought is of all that separates him and sets him apart and makes him different from his creatures. . . . The whole spirit of Old Testament religion was determined by the thought of God's holiness" (J.I. Packer, *Knowing God,* 20th anniversary ed. [Downers Grove, Ill.: InterVarsity Press, 1993], p. 202).

Obviously the sabbath is not "holy" in exactly the same sense that God is holy. We are not told to equate the sabbath with God himself. The sabbath is holy in the sense that it is set apart *from* the remainder of everyday life and *to* God. The word *sacred* carries the same idea.

Question 4. The psalmist finds delight in the Lord (v. 2), in God's people (v.

3) and in God's teaching (v. 7). Ideally we find the same sources of delight as we gather to worship with other Christians in our congregations.

Question 5. "To say 'The Lord is . . . my cup' is to affirm that in sorrow or joy he is the overriding reality" (*New Bible Commentary,* p. 495). The psalmist realizes that God is sovereign over every aspect of his life, and this brings him peace and security.

Question 7. Maintaining an ongoing sense of God's presence is a vital Christian discipline. Believers can do a number of practical things to enhance this attitude, such as placing scriptural reminders on the refrigerator or on the dashboard in the car, keeping Christian music playing in the background or memorizing a verse a week. Perhaps the most effective strategy is to maintain a regular daily quiet time with God.

Questions 9-10. These may be sensitive questions for your group. For many people, even Christians, Sunday has become almost indistinguishable from the other six days of the week. We take time to go to church, but the remainder of the day is often filled with shopping and even with work. The aim of these questions is not to put guilt on those who must work on Sundays. No one wants hospitals, nursing homes, police departments or fire departments to close down one day a week! Most of us, however, have a great deal of freedom about how we spend Sundays.

"[T]he fourth commandment . . . sets aside a portion of time for the worship and service of God as well as for the refreshment and recuperation of human beings. God is the Lord of time. As such, he has a legitimate right to claim a proportion of our time, just as he has a claim on a proportion of our money and our talents" (Walter C. Kaiser Jr., et al., *Hard Sayings of the Bible* [Downers Grove, Ill.: InterVarsity Press, 1996], p. 148).

Study 6. Respect for Parents. Ruth 1:1-18.
Purpose: To discover the value of honoring our parents and to commit ourselves to do so.
General note. Use your knowledge of your group members and their family life to plan your approach to this study. Some study groups include parents and their adult children, which will surely affect the dynamics of your group discussion. Also consider the special challenges facing group members whose parents seem less than honorable.
Question 1. One possibility is that obedience to parents is the first issue a person faces in his or her lifespan. So it would precede the other five "social" commandments for chronological reasons. But there is at least one other reason. "The obligations of son [or daughter] to parents is a deeply religious one

and comes to be used to describe the relation between Israel and her God (Jer. 31:30; Hos. 11:1). This commandment thus provides a good 'bridge' between the two parts of the Ten Commandments" (*The Interpreter's Dictionary of the Bible,* pp. 569-70). It is a "segue" commandment, in other words.

Question 3. Paul calls the fifth commandment "the first commandment with a promise—that it may go well with you and that you may enjoy long life on the earth" (Eph 6:2-3).

This commandment does not offer us a deal or a tradeoff with God. It is more like a law of common sense. Those who respect and revere the elderly are enhancing the environment for their own retirement. Our children are likely to treat us with the same respect after they are grown that they saw us give to their grandparents. Also, we all have a real need to tap into the accumulated wisdom of the previous generation.

Question 5. Like any good parent (and remember that Naomi has had, and lost, two sons), Naomi puts the children's welfare before her own. The prospects of remarriage would be much better for the young women in their own country. Given the difficulties and dangers of Naomi's journey, and the fact that the two girls are the last of her family, she is making a considerable sacrifice. Clearly Naomi is a "parent" worthy of honor.

Question 6. As one who has outlived her husband and even her own children, Naomi understandably feels there has been little providence for her. "The Lord's hand has gone out against me!" is a very human response. Group members should understand that this is another motive for honoring our parents: the years can bring bitterness, and our forebears are worthy of the loving care that can take the sting out. They have done so for us often enough.

Question 8. Ruth parts ways with her sister-in-law Orpah, who would be a more logical companion than her older, foreign mother-in-law. Ruth leaves her homeland and casts her uncertain lot in a strange country. She chooses the dangers of travel. Ruth and Naomi are dual models of the choice of wisdom over expedience.

Question 9. Adults whose parents are aging face difficult decisions about their loyalties and the extent of their responsibility to their parents. Genesis 2:24 indicates that the parent-child relationship is not primary over all others and should not come between a husband and wife. Yet Exodus 20:12 still stands: "Honor your father and your mother." This may be a good time for group members to express concerns and support each other with stories of their own experiences.

Question 10. This passage is often quoted in marriage ceremonies. While the words express a beautiful sentiment for husband and wife, their original context was that of daughter-in-law and mother-in-law!

Question 12. As our population ages, we display conflicting attitudes toward older people. Some think of them as hopelessly behind the times and in the way. Some prefer to ignore them. Some acknowledge their valuable part in society as they stay healthy and active well into their senior years. Some discern their great value as human beings even if their mental and physical powers are gone. Some target them as potential consumers of health products and luxury housing. In general, our culture still idolizes youth and has trouble accepting old age as a fact of life.

Good follow-up questions would be, "What do you know of attitudes toward the elderly in other cultures? What are some similarities and contrasts with our own attitudes?"

Question 13. Creative ways to honor our elders are not difficult to find. A good start might be a greeting card with a warm, personal note of gratitude on a special day—or a nonspecial one. The best expression of love is often time, and we can find extra time to spend with parents or other "significant elders." We need to reflect on the sacrifices made for us by those who have gone before and verbalize our appreciation while there is still time.

Study 7. Respect for Life. 1 Samuel 24.

Purpose: To discover the godly value of life and commit ourselves to respecting it however possible.

Background. Saul became Israel's first king (1 Sam 9—10). Despite his considerable gifts and a strong start, his reign quickly deteriorated. He never grasped that God was still the nation's ultimate ruler. Saul's subjects began to transfer their affections to the young hero David, who had defeated the giant Goliath and had already been anointed as Saul's successor (1 Sam 16). Saul quite naturally felt threatened by his perceived usurper. The palace divided into political factions. To Saul's distress, even his own son Jonathan remained loyal to David (1 Sam 20:30-33). As 1 Samuel 24 begins, Saul is pursuing David with intent to kill.

Question 1. The fewer the words, the more serious the tone communicated. These acts are strictly forbidden; in many cases they brought the death penalty in ancient Israel. This is a good place to note, however, that the Hebrew idea of murder is differentiated from the killing involved in capital punishment or war (see Cole, *Exodus,* pp. 159-60). Arguments against those concepts must be made from the New Testament, of course. This note from *Hard Sayings of the Bible* is helpful: "The Hebrew language possesses seven words related to killing, and the word used in this sixth commandment appears only forty-seven times in the Old Testament. This Hebrew verb, *rasah*, refers only to the killing of a person, never to killing animals, and not even to killing persons in a war. It carries no implications of the means of killing" (*Hard Sayings of the Bible*, p. 148).

Question 3. It is unclear when or how the Lord gave the assurance of verse 4, but clearly David's friends believed the Lord had promised it. The NIV footnote gives an alternate reading: "Today the Lord is saying . . ."

Question 5. David knew he was destined by God to be king of Israel. The prophet Samuel had already anointed him as Saul's successor (1 Sam 16:13). He may have heard directly from Samuel that God had torn the kingdom from Saul and given it to one better (1 Sam 15:28). David knew firsthand from Jonathan that Saul was out to kill him. He knew that Saul had even killed the priests of the Lord who aided David in his flight (1 Sam 22). The opportunity in the cave looked like the perfect time for David to move God's plans along to a tidy conclusion.

Question 6. Saul has gone into the cave to relieve himself (v. 3). David commits a rather infantile practical joke when he violates Saul's privacy, sneaks up on him and cuts off a piece of his clothing. Saul is still God's anointed king (v. 6) and David is sorry for demeaning him.

Question 7. Remember that David is under Saul's personal death sentence. David chooses to respect life, even when his own life has not been respected! He bows down to Saul (v. 8) and addresses him as "my lord the king" (v. 8), "my master" (v. 10) and "my father" (v. 11). He says he could not bring himself to harm the Lord's anointed even when others urged him to do so (v. 10). David could have used the piece of robe to humiliate Saul and to prove his own bravery. Instead he displays it as evidence of his mercy and his regard for Saul (v. 11).

Question 8. David could have waited quietly in the cave, escaped later and still claimed the moral high ground. Instead he risks his life and emerges from hiding to call to Saul. David does not ask Saul to surrender, only to call off the chase. David builds a case that he is innocent of rebellion and is not out to get Saul (vv. 9, 11-13). He confronts Saul about past wrongs but leaves vengeance to God (v. 12).

Question 9. Instead of elevating himself over Saul, David emphasizes his own lack of importance and vulnerability before the king. To take another's life says that the murderer is more worthy of life than the victim. To respect life means to acknowledge that others have as much right to live as we have. Respect for life means that others are as important as we are—perhaps even more important.

Question 10. When we consider that Saul is there in the desert specifically to find and kill David (v. 2), his response is remarkable. He is overcome by contrition (v. 16). He admits that David has done right and he has done wrong (v. 17). He asks God to bless David (v. 19). He even acknowledges that David will be the legitimate king of Israel (v. 20). He requests an oath that his descendants will receive the same mercy David has shown him. Saul will later return to his old attitudes (1 Sam 26), but for now he gives up the pursuit of David.

Question 11. One of the worst aspects of evildoing is the cycle of vengeance that it sets off. Saul realizes he can't thwart David's ascent, which is clearly God's will; but the best he can do is to prevent the murderous spiral.

Question 12. David's kingship may be a foregone conclusion, but Saul has guaranteed his own future safety and that of his descendants from David's hand. As for David, he has set the tone for a wise and just rule. He has refused to use treachery to secure his fate.

Question 13. In the Sermon on the Mount, Jesus broadened the command "You shall not murder" to even include angry verbal attacks on another person (Mt 5:21-22). Respect for life means far more than refraining from physical murder.

Study 8. Respect for Marriage. 2 Samuel 11.
Purpose: To confirm the danger of adultery and resolve to avoid temptation.
Question 1. The first four commandments concern respect for and faithfulness to God. God is holy, and we speak of "holy matrimony." A spouse merits the same kind of priority, faithfulness and respect on a human scale.

Question 2. The sad progress of David's sin illustrates the truth of James 1:13-15. David sees the woman, which is perhaps unavoidable, but the story implies he *keeps on* looking (v. 2). He actively pursues her by sending someone to inquire about her (v. 3). When he learns she is Uriah's wife, he takes action to acquire her anyway (v. 4). He has sexual relations with her (v. 4). When he learns of her pregnancy, he pulls Uriah off the battlefield to give himself an alibi (v. 6). When Uriah proves too loyal to cooperate, David detains him and tries to get him drunk (vv. 12-13). Uriah still balks, so David issues orders to make sure Uriah dies on the battlefield (v. 14).

A possible follow-up question: At each point of the story, what could David have done to stop the process and avoid sin?

Question 3. The biblical account makes no attempt to hide David's sin nature. We may be disappointed that King David, one of our most beloved heroes, could fall into such a destructive spiral of sin; in much the same way we are also disappointed in ourselves when we face our own sin nature.

Question 4. Adultery is almost always a secret sin, so it necessitates deceit of a spouse (or two). For a Christian it necessitates self-deceit, since the seventh commandment forbids it in such absolute terms. The two adulterers often deceive each other with false promises of marriage at some later date. And while no one can deceive God, a Christian who sets out to commit adultery must at least try to "hide" it from God, perhaps by pious excuses.

Question 5. You may want to allow time for private reflection on this question. In responding people don't have to reveal personal details. You can talk about patterns and temptations.

Question 6. David has claimed a woman who is not his own. Uriah is so dedicated to his life as the king's soldier that he will not even enjoy the woman who is rightfully his own. The contrast between the two makes David's final touch even more chilling. He has Uriah unknowingly deliver his own death warrant—a terrible "reward" for a good soldier and loyal servant. (According to 2 Sam 23:24-39, Uriah the Hittite was one of David's "Thirty," the elite military fighters.)

Question 7. Adultery violates trust between husband and wife. Ironically, when it happens in places of power, it inevitably requires the cooperation of people who can be trusted to keep quiet. David involves his own servants, who inquire about Bathsheba and go to summon her (vv. 3-4). He orders his own army commander, Joab, to deliberately abandon one of his best soldiers to death (v. 15).

Most of all, of course, David pulls Bathsheba into the sin of adultery. We do not know how willingly she complies. David is the king; Bathsheba can hardly refuse him. On the other hand, she bathes within sight of the palace roof. Does she know she can be seen? Is she tired of being married to a soldier who is often away? We can only speculate about the answers.

Question 8. David waits a decent interval and then marries Bathsheba, though she mourns the husband he has slain. It is clear that David has lost his moral compass. He will show no repentance until Nathan's confrontation (2 Sam 12).

Question 9. This question offers an opportunity for a sobering contrast of David the adulterous king with David in the preceding study (1 Sam 24), a young man of humility whose actions seem dictated by conscience. While it is impossible to precisely read David's heart, we can observe that he is now a man in a secure position of power. Perhaps this access to power and luxury has (at least temporarily) dulled David's conscience. The massive proportions of his sin may have blinded him to its gravity. Or David may have been suppressing his guilt.

Question 10. David's sins include coveting, murder, adultery and lying. This would total four of the six "social" commandments.

Question 11. It does no good to pray "Lord, keep me from adultery" and then willingly put ourselves in the way of temptation. We have to take steps (often literal steps, walking away) to avoid morally dangerous situations. Like David, we may not be able to avoid exposure to temptation, but we can choose to turn away (unlike David). No Christian should imagine that he or she is immune from this sin. God knows our hearts, and he promises to give us strength to resist. Helpful Scriptures are 1 Corinthians 6:18-20 and 10:12-13.

Question 12. Consider breaking in pairs to discuss this more personally.

Prayer. Allow time for silent prayer and confession as well as appropriate corporate prayer.

Study 9. Respect for Property. Acts 4:32—5:11.
Purpose: To understand the varieties of stealing and build respect for the property of others.

Question 1. The introduction to this study provides an illustration that might hit a nerve or two. Encourage group members to think of subtle instances of taking what is not one's own. For example, ignoring the right-of-way at a traffic intersection, pirating cable television, taking office supplies home from work or even stealing time through tardiness.

Question 2. The setting is the church in Jerusalem in the first weeks after the outpouring of the Holy Spirit at Pentecost. Acts 2:40-47 gives the background of this infant church.

> The early Christians acknowledge that Jesus owns both them and their property (cf. 4:32); they sell off property to meet needs as they arise (4:34-35) and open their homes as meeting places for fellow Christians (2:46). These actions do not reflect an ascetic ideal, as in some Greek and Jewish sects, but instead the practice of radically valuing people over possessions. . . . [T]he outpouring of God's Spirit here leads not only to miracles and inspired verbal witness but also to actively caring for one another and sharing possessions. (Craig S. Keener, *The IVP Bible Background Commentary: New Testament* [Downers Grove, Ill.: Inter-Varsity Press, 1993], pp. 330, 334)

Question 3. In the world's way of doing things, greed prevails. By contrast, unselfishness and generosity attract positive attention and open people's ears to hear the gospel.

Question 6. Personal ownership is in no way negated. The Christians in Acts retain their possessions but simply share them willingly. Peter makes it clear that the land belonged to Ananias and Sapphira before it was sold, and even after it was sold, the money was theirs to dispose of as they chose (v. 4). "The description of selling one's goods in Acts 2:45 is expanded in Acts 4:34. In both cases the verb tense indicates an ongoing process. Whenever a need came to light, those having goods sold them and brought the money to provide for the need. As if these descriptions were not clear enough, in Acts 5:3-4 the author makes it plain that such generosity was not a legal requirement; it was the lie, not the failure to give, for which Ananias and Sapphira are condemned" (*Hard Sayings of the Bible,* pp. 517-18).

Question 8. Ananias and Sapphira thought they were putting one over on the apostles, but Peter says the lie was actually directed at God. Peter analyzes the situation in light of Satan, the Holy Spirit and God. Those who live in obedience maintain a spiritual perspective on earthly matters.

Question 9. This may be a troubling question for group members. It is important to consider the context: the church in Acts is in its infancy. The future of Christianity rests with the "charter members." Maintaining purity is absolutely essential. The weed of sin is extracted before it can spread, and a solemn message is communicated.

Study 10. Respect for the Truth. Proverbs 12.
Purpose: To discover the damage of dishonesty and to seek personal integrity.
Question 1. The commandments are arranged, in roughly descending order of severity, from our regard for God, to our treatment of God, to our behavior among ourselves, to our words and thoughts. The last two commandments—concerning lying and coveting—fall into the final category. This does not mean lying is a sin of low magnitude; but in many situations it might be less damaging in its effect on others than murder, adultery and stealing. Coveting might never affect another person directly.

Question 3. Honest words can vindicate someone who has been slandered. Honest testimony can bring about justice for someone unfairly accused of a crime. An honest expression of confidence can lift the spirit, perhaps even save the life, of someone who feels beaten down by circumstances.

Question 5. Among other things, our words affect those around us and partly determine how others perceive us and receive us. The person who uses speech positively and productively creates a healthful atmosphere.

The second part of the question emphasizes the fact that words and work (the two themes of this section of the Proverbs) are inseparable. The godly person both speaks and acts in truth.

Question 6. The writer's concern is not simply truth as an abstract consideration; rather, he warns of how we can destroy others and ourselves through our words. Lying and ill-considered statements both come from a heart out of sync with God's ways.

Question 7. The short answer is "yes." One can indeed speak the truth recklessly. Paul tells us to speak the truth in love (Eph 4:15). Some use the truth as a weapon. Again, biblical writers do not discuss truth in the abstract; the important thing is always our standing with God and each other.

Question 10. Lying promotes Satan's chief desire: to separate humanity from God's truth. Dishonesty alienates us from God and from each other. A lie, especially by a Christian, is a success for Satan.

Study 11. The Value of Contentment. 1 Timothy 6:3-10.

Purpose: To gain an understanding of the nature and effect of coveting and to strive for "godliness with contentment."

Question 1. Coveting is a "gateway sin" which leads to many other commandment violations. In fact, it could lead to violation of any or all of the other nine commandments. Obedience to this final word serves as "preventive maintenance" for the others. See also the note for study 10, question 1.

An accurate understanding of the word *covet* is essential for this study. The Hebrew word is *desire,* which is not sin in itself; the key distinction is that when the object is something owned by someone else, desire becomes covetousness.

Question 2. One possibility: A "thought crime" needs to be fleshed out in practical, physical terms for the hearers. Also, the examples demonstrate the breadth of the implications of this commandment.

Question 4. In this letter Paul frequently deals with teachers of heresy. Some of these teachers have taken the classic teaching that those who follow God's law tend to prosper and have distorted it into false religion with a profit motive. Wealth is a reasonable, possible byproduct of godliness, not the incentive for it.

Question 5. Contentment is an outgrowth of godliness. Becoming godly nurtures God's perspective within us. We realize that in him we have everything we need.

Question 6. Godly contentment goes beyond enjoyment of the status quo. Liberation from material longing is a spiritual step forward. It is indeed great gain.

Question 8. Covetousness begins with a basic dissatisfaction with how God has treated us. We do not simply look at a beautiful car or a beautiful person and demand, "I have to have that." First we experience a nagging unhappiness with what we have. Then we look around for whatever will fill our supposed need. Other people's possessions, relationships and good fortune look so much better than what God has chosen to give us. We feel cheated and demand our fair share.

Question 10. Christians can be fully content and happy with their lot in life, yet still have ambitions for other reasonable goals. The vital questions are Does God come first in our heart? Does godliness define and direct our ambitions?

Question 11. In *Money Isn't God,* John White writes: "The god of greed is a cheat. His promise of material rewards may never even be kept. He cheats his priests as much as he cheats his worshipers, turning his back on both and leaving them to their despair once he no longer has use for them. And even those upon whom he lavishes his rewards find them strangely flat. His flowers are made of plastic and his food of sawdust, while his wine can neither refresh nor intoxicate. His delights have the power to dazzle and excite, but they can satisfy nobody" ([Downers Grove, Ill.: InterVarsity Press, 1993], pp. 147-48).

Study 12. The Law of Grace. Romans 3:9-31.
Purpose: To consider the relationship between law and grace, and to deepen our security in Christ's redeeming grace.

General note. For some Christians, this study will seem basic; for newer believers, it will be complex. Be sure to thoroughly review Romans 3 (and, for context, Romans 2) before the study. Be ready to explain terms like *atonement, grace* and *justification.*

Question 1. Despite the fact that the Jews were entrusted with God's law (see 3:1), in the end there is no distinction between the two. Everyone has offended God; the law itself cannot save anyone, Jew or Gentile; and everyone must come to God for forgiveness on the same basis: through Christ.

Question 4. The power of sin extends to all humanity. We are "under sin" in the sense that through our human abilities we cannot avoid sin's daily damage. By "the law" Jews understand that there are specific works found in God's law which are requirements for pleasing God. Apart from Christ, all people are subject to the cycle of sin's power and the law's requirements.

Question 7. *Righteousness* refers to an individual's conformity with God's laws. *Justification* is meeting that standard and being declared innocent. *Grace* is God's generous action to us above and beyond what justice would require. *Redemption* is the payment of a required price to free or obtain something.

Question 10. A Jewish reader of this letter might be proud of his faithfulness to the law. Paul, through his argument, shows the folly of boasting when human righteousness (apart from grace) is impossible.

Question 11. Before grace came to us, attempting to live by God's law seemed futile. With the perspective of grace, we can begin to obey God's commandments and uphold the law, confident that he has already accepted us.

Rob Suggs is a freelance writer living in Atlanta, Georgia. He is also the author of the LifeGuide® Bible Study Christian Community.

What Should We Study Next?

A good place to continue your study of Scripture would be with a book study. Many groups begin with a Gospel such as *Mark* (20 studies by Jim Hoover) or *John* (26 studies by Douglas Connelly). These guides are divided into two parts so that if twenty or twenty-six weeks seems like too much to do at once, the group can feel free to do half and take a break with another topic. Later you might want to come back to it. You might prefer to try a shorter letter. *Philippians* (9 studies by Donald Baker), *Ephesians* (11 studies by Andrew T. and Phyllis J. Le Peau) and *1 & 2 Timothy and Titus* (11 studies by Pete Sommer) are good options. If you want to vary your reading with an Old Testament book, consider *Ecclesiastes* (12 studies by Bill and Teresa Syrios) for a challenging and exciting study.

There are a number of interesting topical LifeGuide studies as well. Here are some options for filling three or four quarters of a year:

Basic Discipleship
Christian Beliefs, 12 studies by Stephen D. Eyre
Christian Character, 12 studies by Andrea Sterk & Peter Scazzero
Christian Disciplines, 12 studies by Andrea Sterk & Peter Scazzero
Evangelism, 12 studies by Rebecca Pippert & Ruth Siemens

Building Community
Christian Community, 10 studies by Rob Suggs
Fruit of the Spirit, 9 studies by Hazel Offner
Spiritual Gifts, 12 studies by Charles & Anne Hummel

Character Studies
David, 12 studies by Jack Kuhatschek
New Testament Characters, 12 studies by Carolyn Nystrom
Old Testament Characters, 12 studies by Peter Scazzero
Women of the Old Testament, 12 studies by Gladys Hunt

The Trinity
Meeting God, 12 studies by J. I. Packer
Meeting Jesus, 13 studies by Leighton Ford
Meeting the Spirit, 12 studies by Douglas Connelly